This book is dedicated to all girls -
you are brave, you are powerful and you are tough.
You can accomplish anything you put your mind to.

ISBN: 979-8-218-05679-7

For more books, visit us online at empowerbooksforkids.net

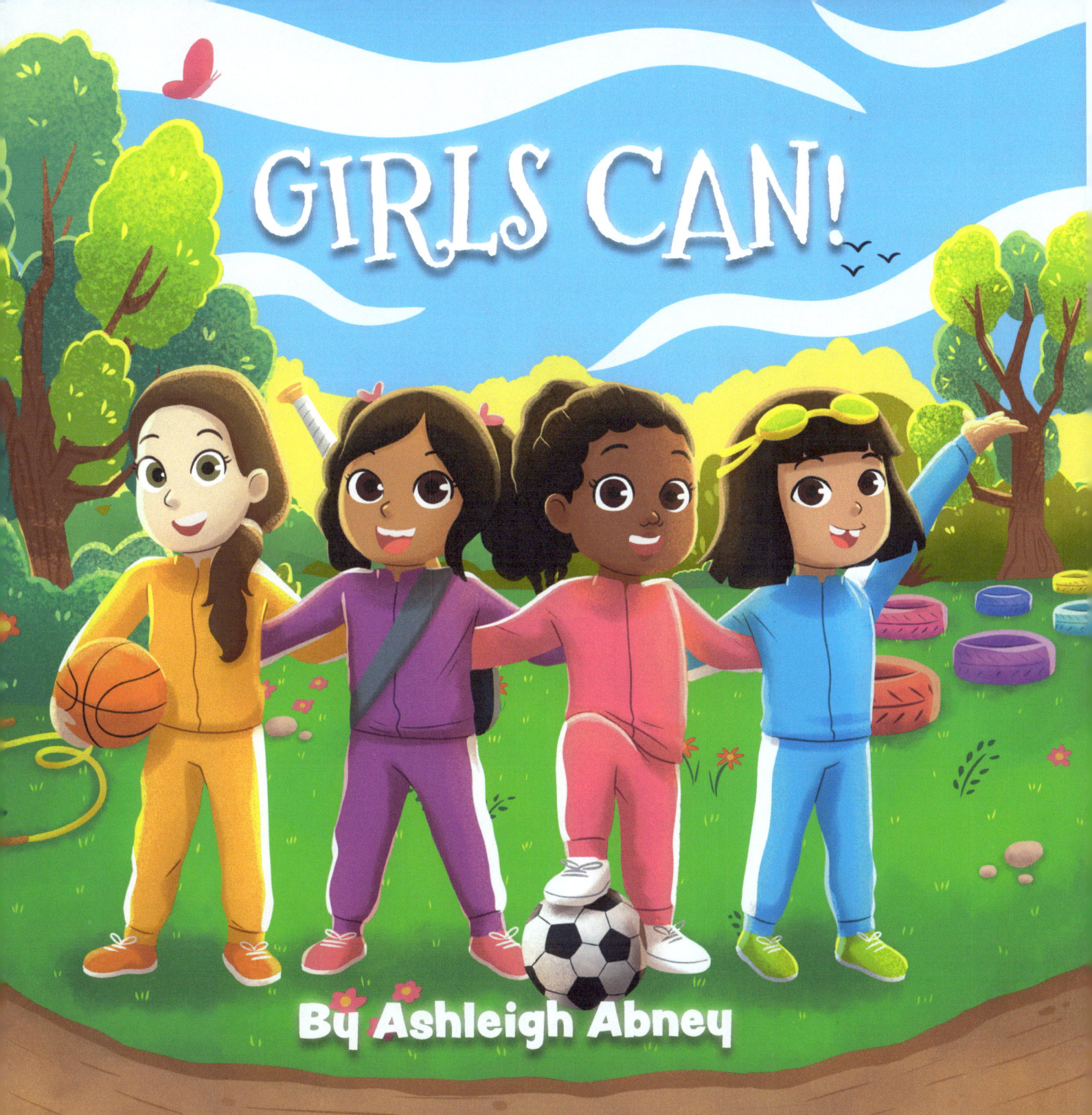

Being a girl is so fun!

We love to **play** and **skip** and **run**.

We can play any sport we set our **minds** to...

Whether it is lacrosse, volleyball,
or anything the boys **can** do.

We are **fierce** and we are **tough!**

We can **tumble** and do all kinds of **stuff.**

Maybe basketball is your favorite...
bounce, bounce, bounce.

Practice your dribbling — that's what really **counts.**

Cheerleading is **fun**, and you can pump up the **fans**.

We jump, flip, and dance as they clap their hands.

1	29.5 s.
2	30.6 s.
3	31.8 s.

On your mark, get set, go!

As you race around the track...

The one who is the fastest will be first to get **back**.

Is soccer your sport? Girls can do that too!

We can **shoot** and **score**.
Yes, one day that can be **you.**

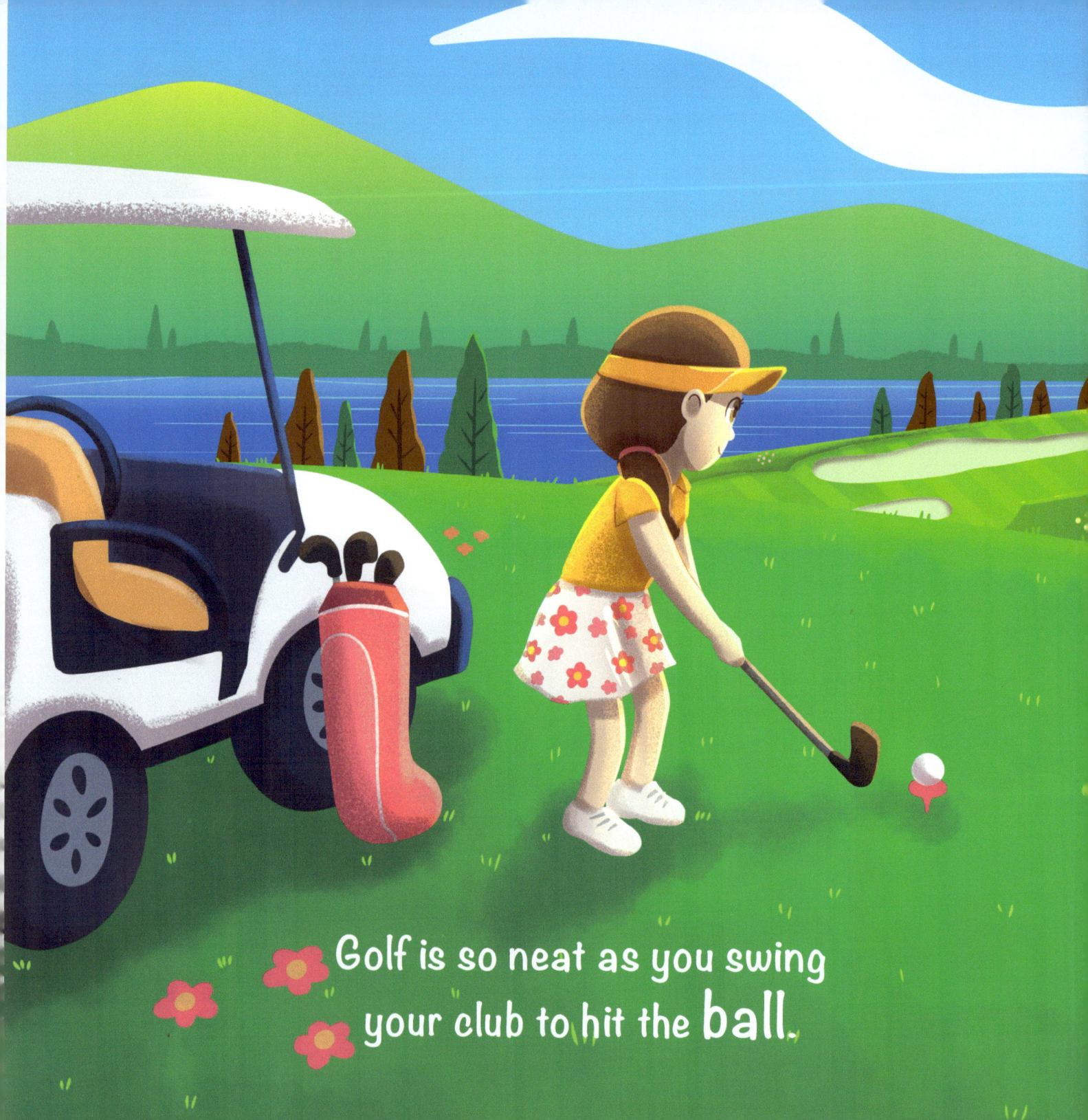

Golf is so neat as you swing your club to hit the **ball**.

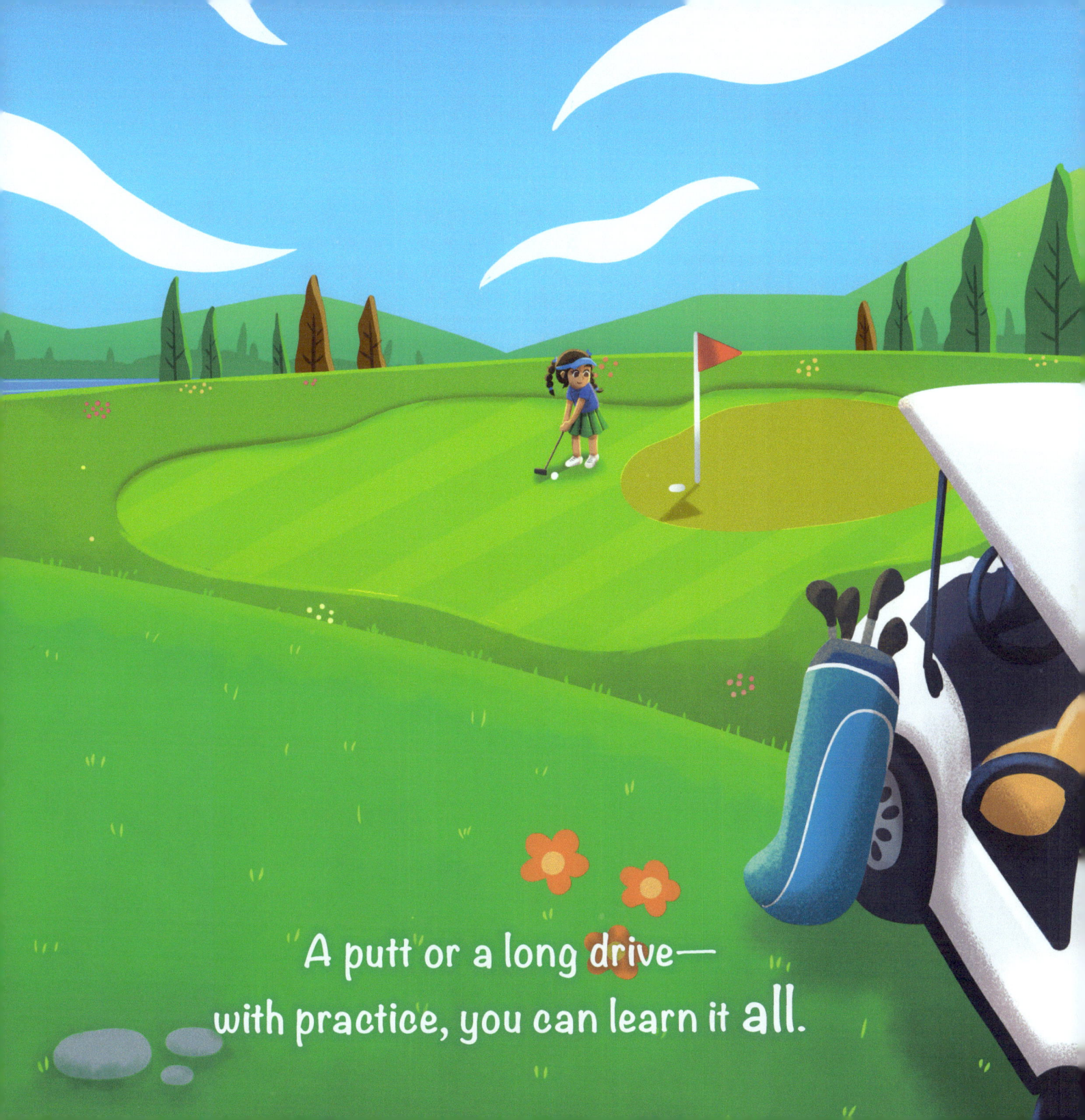

A putt or a long drive—
with practice, you can learn it all.

Swimming is awesome. As we play in the pool ...

We can **float**, swim really **fast**, or even compete. That's so **cool**.

Give tennis a try. So many amazing women play ...

They serve the **ball** so fast.
You can do that too one **day**.

But don't forget softball! It's so much fun.

Swing your bat, go to first base,
or maybe one day you'll hit a home run!

Pick your sport and go have fun
so you can be a **star**...

It just takes practice but know
you **can** do it just the way you **are**.

The Education Amendments Act of 1972 transformed Women's Sports. Title IX enabled women athletes to have the right to equal opportunity in educational institutions that receive federal funds – this includes elementary schools to colleges and universities.

Title IX states:

"No person in the United States shall, on the basis of sex, be excluded from participation in, be denied the benefits of, or be subjected to discrimination under any education program or activity receiving federal financial assistance."

The groundbreaking gender equity law made a lasting impact by increasing the participation of girls and women in athletics.

About the Author

Ashleigh has always had a competitive spirit and passion for sports. As a former college basketball player, she often reflects on the benefits sports contributed to her life. The lessons learned through sports inspired her to find a way to encourage young girls to "get in the game."

Girls drop out of sports at twice the rate of boys and we should strive to change this. She hopes this book will motivate parents to encourage their children to give sports a try as studies show many critical benefits such as improved physical/mental health, confidence, leadership, fun and so much more!

Stay connected for more books from the Empower Books collection.

 EmpowerBooks   Empower_Books

empowerbooksforkids.net

www.ingramcontent.com/pod-product-compliance
Lightning Source LLC
Chambersburg PA
CBHW041444120626
46547CB00002B/346